Learn the Secrets of Shaping Your Best Shape

&

Doing It Yourself!

DANA BURKS

This book is a general educational health-related information product and is intended for healthy adults ages 18 and over. Not all exercises are suitable for everyone, and this or any exercise program may result in injury.

Any specific results mentioned in this book should be considered exceptional, as there are no "typical" results. As individuals vary, results will differ.

Please consult with your doctor before you use any suggestion found within this book. To reduce the risk of injury, never force or strain yourself during any exercise. If you feel pain, stop immediately and seek medical attention, if necessary.

Those with special health considerations should consult their doctor before performing any exercise. The information found within this book is given in good faith and is neither intended to diagnose any physical or mental condition nor to serve as a substitute for informed and medical advice or care. Please contact your health care professional for medical advice and treatment.

Neither the author of this book or any resources mentioned can be held liable by any person for any loss or damage whatsoever which may arise from the use of this book. If you are new to exercise in general, I strongly recommend getting a knowledgeable professional personal trainer. Even the slightest injury can lead to a domino effect of injuries that may affect the achieving of your goals. Please follow this program with care and at your own risk.

Mention of specific companies, organizations or authorities in this book does imply endorsement by the author or publisher, nor does mention of specific companies, organizations or authorities imply that they endorse this book, its author, or the publisher. Internet addresses, emails, and telephone numbers mentioned in this book were accurate at the time it went to publish

Self M.I.L.F Made © 2016 Dana Burks

Photographs & Images © 2016 by iStockPhoto, Eric Burks, & Dana Fontanoza Burks

Self M.I.L.F. Made is a pending registered trademark of Body Reign.

Visit the author's website:
www.DanaBurks.com

For the selfless ladies who give and give and give... the sisters, the daughters, the aunties, the grandmas, the mommies... may you find this book useful and may the patience to persevere, the tenacity to keep moving forward, and the stubbornness of loving overflow from within... may success of overall health: mind, body, and soul, be yours, always!

For my daughters... Maura, Madelyn, Mia, & Megan... without you, I wouldn't be the person I am today. I wouldn't trade anything for being blessed with giving birth to each of you and being your mommy. Thank you. I love each of you... more than you know.

Acknowledgments

I have honestly been blessed with the most encouraging people. With heartfelt thanks to these awesome beings that have shared their energy and undying support, I thank you. Especially....

My clients- previous & current... unknowingly, you helped make all this happen... thank you!!!

My biggest cheerleaders, Roslyn and Lizzy... Thank you for being the constant voice telling me "Do it!!!"

My most awesome cousins, Millicent, Sesi, & Maureen for your unconditional love and support.

My dad, for your wise words when I was little and introducing me to aging with grace through caring for myself. I really hope those kids in those countries are happy because I ate all my vegetables :)

My godfather, Marshall, never leaving my side from the day I was born. You taught me to work/love hard and to stay the course of your dreams, no matter what. I am. Thanks to your example.

My mother, Aurora, you taught me to do everything with good intentions and not care about what anyone was thinking. Thank you for telling me "You always gotta do what's right. You gotta do it from your heart! And don't care what anyone thinks. If they don't like it, they can shove it up their ASS!" haha I love you, mommy.

My eldest daughters, Maura & Madelyn... thank you so much for allowing me to do what I needed to do to get things done. Your taking initiative, helping out in every which way that you can, and for not changing despite all that we've been through... I hope to make you as proud as you have made me. I love all my girls, so much.

And to my helluva sexy man, my knight in shining armor... With your strength, crazy love, & rock solid devotion to my every existence. You have not only awaken my creative spirit, but unknowingly you have been the missing link to everything I needed to constantly be reminded of being unafraid to complete my circles. Who needs superheroes when I've got you.... I love you, Eric.

Table of Contents

Preface

Just like a makeup artist applies primer before applying any makeup, or a contractor preps the ground before even pouring the concrete for the foundation, we have to prepare our minds to take care of our bodies.

Why would I want to take care of my body or get it in its best shape possible, anyway?

What exactly is my best shape?

What if my genetics made my body the way it is?

First of all, you can Google your heart out and learn that we can alter our own DNA just by changing what we expose ourselves to.

This could be through the food we eat and the "*foods*" we feed our minds!

I would cover all the health journals I've read, but that's a totally different book in itself!

For now, I'd like to cover the reason why it's so important for you to *want* to take care of yourself, to not only feel good, but to be naturally aesthetically appealing, too!

Our primal instinct is to attract a mate.

Unfortunately, in today's judgmental society, you are damned if you do and damned if you don't for any of your efforts.

What you allow into your mind whether through the people you hang out with, the books you read, and even the television shows you watch, can alter your thinking.

So many people grow up thinking one way is right, when their parents did it, and their parents parents did it, and so on and so forth.

For example: Frying all your food in lard, which is what your family does or did whilst preparing meals.

This creates the story in your mind of how you think what is *right for you*.

When we are "*taught*" to live a certain way and wonder why we can't be in the best shape we could possibly be in, we wonder why we are depressed and unable to reach our desired goals, no matter if they are physically, mentally, or financially.

It's because we are at war with what we've been "*taught*" versus what our natural human instincts are.

Since our primal instinct is to mate and procreate. Our natural human instincts are to be attracted to what is sexually appealing.

In turn, this makes perfect sense to *want* to be attractive or sexually appealing for ourselves in order to attract the mate we desire!

Then we are left with the question of how can you be or find yourself appealing if you can't get past yourself?

Being at war with ourselves is truly a vicious cycle.

This is where you have to make a truly conscientious decision and tell yourself that it's time to think for yourself, and break free from what is the "norm" in today's society and your environment.

Be You!

This is **your** body, these should be *your* rules, naturally!

This rings *especially* true if you believe that just because diabetes and disease runs in your family, that it has to run in you, too.

It doesn't.

Welcome!

Before we continue, I'd like to take a moment to congratulate you on taking matters into your own hands!

While we were born with the bodies we currently live in, there actually are factors that can trump over genetics.

Among these factors are age, hormones, living conditions, your environment, and even your day to day activities.

In this guide, you will learn about your unique body shape and explore my tried and true techniques that I've used on myself and my clients!

As a mother of four children and nearing my 40's, believe me when I say, I UNDERSTAND.

I went from a pretty average, healthy teenager to an overweight adult. From there I tried different workout videos and various dieting methods. My favorites were Billy Blanks, Denise Austin, and Tamilee Webb.

From overweight I then went to skinny fat.

This frustrating cycle would happen two more times, until I figured out what I really needed to do to get the body that I wanted.

I knew that being skinny could not be right based on the way that my clothes would fit me and how I was out of breath and could easily be tackled and taken down by my then 8-year-old when play wrestling.

I began looking into weightlifting and then combined the methods I had learned from watching my father and uncles exercising, other trainers, and of course formal education.

I knew I was on to something when I noticed that my body bounced back much quicker after having my last child.

Upon becoming a personal trainer, and watching my clients' bodies change right before my eyes, I can honestly say that I truly believe that I have found my calling.

Unfortunately, life would have me move away from my clients on two occasions. Also, since this was my only method of bringing home the bacon and paying my bills whilst being there for my children as a single mom, I did notice not many other moms could really afford my services.

But I still want to help!

With great pride I would like to welcome you to
Self M.I.L.F. Made!

I wish you positive vibes with all your health goals and self-mastery endeavors.

In good health, love, and light...

Dana Burks

P.S. Be sure to read the Final Notes at the back of this book, before you begin your program!

Why M.I.L.F.?!

I used to be oblivious to comments I'd hear while picking up my teenager from school, "Oh your mom's a MILF!"

At first, I honestly thought, "Well, that's awkwardly flattering."

Uh, little boys, I am your friend's mom. So I am old enough to be *your* mom!

For a second, I thought I should dress more my age. Ditch the skinny jeans and heels, and opt for the saggy booty mommy pants... Heck, maybe the other moms would like me better.

I then began to think, why the heck do I have to downplay my self image and how I wanted to dress for the sake of others and how they were perceiving me.

Ummm... No, thank you.

I played the haggard frumpy mom long enough after having had four beautiful babies and was a stay at home mom for many parts of it.

That sweats sporting, no make up, not wanting to care for myself, because everyone was put first and there was not enough time for eyebrows or mascara, we had to go- woman had to go, too!

MILF Confessions here... I wanted to be that sexy and confidant woman I used to be and faintly remembered.

I low key really liked being called a MILF... just wished it was from older men. haha

In reality, I low key really liked knowing that my efforts from being the Disheveled Dana everyone was so used to seeing was actually breaking free and becoming the magnificent spirit animal of her own right!

Unless you've been living under a rock before 1999, I'm pretty sure you've heard the term "MILF" before.

Since then, and with the help of the internet and social media, women of all ages, statuses, whether mom or not, have been subject to even more stereotypes.

This categorizing of women has allowed others to call us names and put us in these assumptions of how others *"think"* we women, actually are.

In so many ways, many of us have put ourselves down to bring others up. We allow our sparkle to dull or we simply put ourselves on the back burner so that others can shine.

Many of us allow these ill connotations, because it seems the norm.

What I'd like to see, and other women like me would like to see, is *ALL* women being self-empowered and unafraid to take care of #1.

Strong is the new sexy! But not only physically, mentally, too!

For me personally, I really enjoy looking like and being a woman, curves and all.

If you're with me, then read on!

But first, let me further explain, in Self MILF Made, "M-I-L-F" stands for Moms Into Lifting and Fitness.

While "Fitness" is a lifestyle that will be approached with baby steps within this book, "Lifting" is a method of building the body with either weights or increasing intensity using resistance.

This program is **for moms** and **future moms** or what my girlfriends call *"Mamasita's"*.

Together, let's change the negative connotation that just because we want to be sexy, that we just want sexual attention.

We actually want more than that.

We want to be strong, smart,
AND sexy...
and in every which way...
and surprisingly, *not* for attention.

We want it ALL for our own self-worth.

Which, quite frankly, is so much more valuable than *any* attention we can get outside of ourselves.

With self-worth we allow ourselves to become so full of love and inner strength that it overflows and our loved ones can't help but follow suit.

Remember, our outsides reflect our insides and vice versa.

I encourage you to embrace the strength in all of your curves, mentally, physically, and everything else that makes You!

Your Goals

So you want nice legs?

Maybe you want to work on your arms more than your legs?

Perhaps, you just feel like an overhaul will do you justice.

Whatever your fitness goals are, exercise and nutrition need to go hand in hand.

While I cannot guarantee your results, because your dedication to your own transformation, any change is entirely up to you!

Through seeing results with my own clients, I can assure you that if you follow even just a few of these suggestions that I've provided in the following pages, you will notice a difference.

Make your Goals **S.M.A.R.T.** Use the SMM Workbook!

Also, I strongly recommend that you get a fitness journal to chart your progress or use the pages of the SMM workbook. Printable templates are provided on-line at www.bodyreign.com.

Ready?!

You got this!

Lets' Go!

Making My Goals S.M.A.R.T.

SMART is a mnemonic acronym used by many in any goal getting industry.

It merely stands for Specific, Measurable, Achievable, Relevant, and Time-Bound.

While you can easily make up your own SMART way, the following is to help you get started:

My goals are:

I am doing this for:

Why am I a doing this...

I want to lose/gain this amount of weight:

My body inspiration is the best version of me, but _____, inspires me, too!

I'm going to commit _____days and _____hour(s) in these days to get to my goals.

I want to achieve my goals by this date:

and check my progress every: week/month/3months?

"When I get up and work out,
I'm working out just as much for my girls
as I am for me, because I want them to see a
mother who loves them dearly, who invests in them,
but who also invests in herself.

It's just as much about letting them know as young
women that it is okay to put yourself a little higher
on your priority list."

~Michelle Obama

YOUR SHAPE

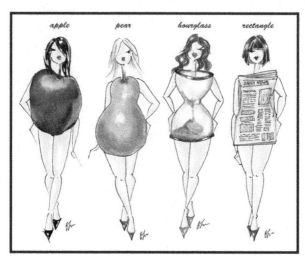

Your Shape:
Finding Your Body Shape

Like fashion trends, body types apparently go in and out of style, too! It's crazy, right?!

You'd think that with bodies, they're just bodies and that's all there is to it! Just like a piece of paper is a piece of paper.

Oh, but then you soon learn that there are different kinds of paper, and different paper weights, even!

 That in itself is an entirely new conversation!

Can you recall a model by the name of Kate Moss? She was really big during her prime.   During the early 90's, the waif model, and that body frame was all the rage! Women of all ages and races were starving themselves to obtain what the masses were calling "ideal".

Now a day, with everything in the media, it is apparent that the hourglass or even the pear shaped body types are what's on everyone's radar.

When clients come to me for their first training session and we go over their goals, the majority of my female clients have told me that they want to: have a "nice booty", small waist, and toned arms.

Later throughout the consultation, I soon learn that they would like to have their bodies looking along the lines of Beyonce or Kim Kardashian, and even myself. (Me?! Really?!)

With that said, in the following pages you will learn that MILF Making is geared towards balancing the body you have and working specific muscle groups to reach the tight curvy aka healthy hourglass shape (whilst avoiding the manly box shape every woman has told me they would like to avoid!).

Just think of taking a stick doll and placing just enough modeling clay on the parts where we'd like to see accentuated.

Do not worry about fat loss, as fat loss will happen.

One thing we want to remember:
We want unhealthy fat loss and not just weight loss!

Before we continue, at any time during this program or any time for that matter, please do not beat yourself up mentally if you find that you are not starting at fitness level or the the shape that you thought you were.

Many women would like to believe that she is an hourglass body type to begin with.

Research in 2005 (source: Dr. Istook & AlvaProducts) found that only a small 8% of the 6,000 plus female body types that were scanned, were actually in the hourglass category.

I'll put the percentage of their findings near the body shape name so that you can see where your own body type falls amongst the majority of the bodies scanned.

You might be surprised!

First,
Choose the body shape
that best describes your own
body...

Hourglass
Triangle
Pear
Apple
Ruler/Brick
Petite

A. Hourglass (8.40%)

Your body shape if:
Hips, bust, are around the same size or with measurements within 5% of each other. Waist is relatively small in comparison or 25% smaller than your hip and bust measurement. While your shoulders may seem droopy, your bum is known to be rather nice to begin with. Your weight is gained in your hips and above the waist.

A Few Famous Hourglasses: Sophia Loren, Marilyn Monroe, Elizabeth Taylor, Lynda Carter, & Beyonce

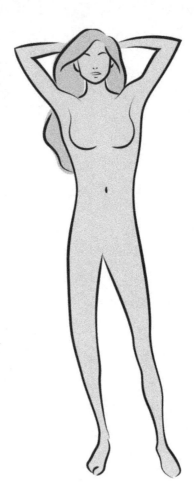

B. Triangle (13.83%)

Your body shape if: Shoulders are more than 5% bigger than your hip measurement. Your broad shoulders are wider than your waistline or hips. You probably have some work to do in the derrière department. Your weight is most likely gained throughout your torso and back.

A Few Famous Triangles: Catherine Zeta-Jones, Charlize Theron, Teri Thatcher, & Pamela Anderson

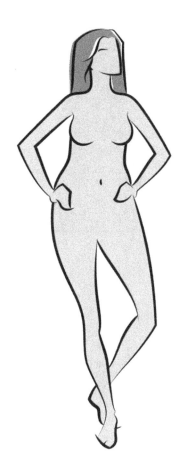

C. Pear (20.92%)

Your body shape if: Hips are more than 5% bigger than your shoulder or bust measurement. Your shoulders are narrow with a tiny waist. You probably have some work to do in the arms and upper back department. Your weight is most likely gained throughout your hips and thighs.

A Few Famous Pears: Beyonce, Jennifer Lopez, Kate Winslet & Shakira

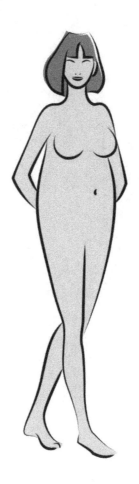

D. **Apple** (13.83%)

Your body shape if: Hips, waist, and chest have very close measurements. Your legs and arms may be very slender and your thighs and hips may be the narrowest part of your body. Your high hip is wider than your lower hip. Your waist might be short. Your weight gain happens dominantly around your waist.

A Few Famous Apples: Tyra Banks, Angelina Jolie, Elizabeth Hurley, & Jennifer Hudson

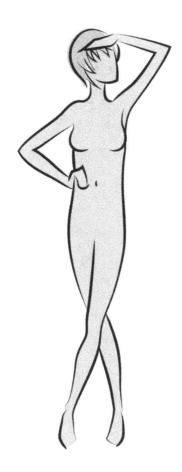

E. Ruler (46.12%)

Your shape if: your hips, waistline, and shoulders measure about the same width. Your shoulders may be straight and broad. Like the Triangle, you have an athletic build and small bust line. Your weight gain is evenly, but may be dominant through your neck and upper back. Most likely ectomorph built.

A Few Famous Rulers: Reese Witherspoon, Keira Knightly, & Nicole Kidman

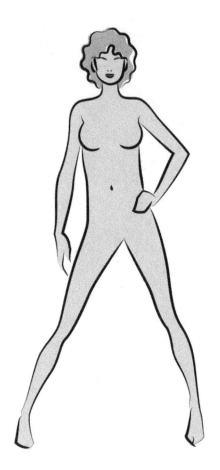

F. Brick (46.12%)

Your shape if: your hips, waistline, and shoulders measure about the same width. Your shoulders may be straight and broad. Like the Triangle, you have an athletic build and small bust line. Your weight gain is evenly, but may be dominant through your neck and upper back. Most likely endomorph built.

A Few Famous Bricks: Cameron Diaz, Sheryl Crow, & Hillary Duff

G. Petite (% N/A, but represent 70% of the female population in the US. Source: Bellapetite)

This is your shape, if you are 5'5" tall or under. Your body type would be petite plus the body shape that best describes your body now according to the previous body shape descriptions.

A Few Famous Petites: Lady Gaga (5'1), Nicole Richie (5'1), & Jada Pinkett Smith (5'0)

"Women who seek to be
    equal with men lack ambition."
                                    ~Timothy Leary

YOUR BODY SHAPING NEEDS

A. Hourglass

You tend to build muscle
faster overall. You will
NOT need to add weights
in the beginning of your
program until you've
reached your desired goal
for any fat loss. High reps
with low to medium
resistance/intensity. Avoid
leg bulking exercises until
reaching your ideal fat loss
goal. Stretching and SMR
is beneficial to avoid injury
and the *appearance* of
being shorter.

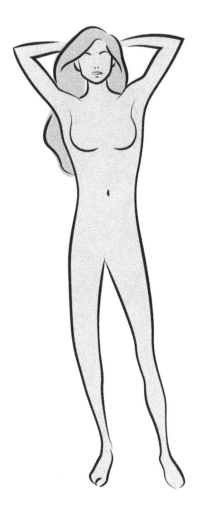

B. Triangle

You will need to add medium to heavy resistance training to your lower body to balance your shoulders. Your Arms Day will be much lighter with high reps and your Booty Days will be the exact opposite. For Booty Days focus on building your gluteus medius to create more hips (Abductor Exercises!).

C. Pear

Like the Hourglass, you will not need weights during your Booty/Leg Days until you've reached your desired goal for fat loss, but medium to heavy weights can be used on your Arms Days. Booty/ Leg Days will also be focused on high reps. Stretching and SMR may be beneficial to avoid injury and the appearance of being shorter.

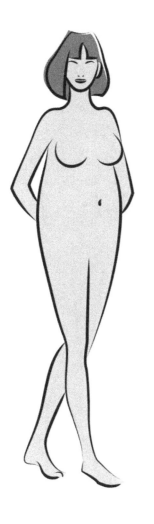

D. Apple

Your days will focus on resistance based cardio, like stair climbing and plyometric exercises like burpees. We'll need to focus on exercises that focus on your whole body with specified extremities, for instance jumping jacks paired with weighted squats followed by various style planks. Once your desired fat loss is obtained, more heavy weights and higher resistance can be used to further build your less dominant body parts, like arms and thighs.

E./F. Ruler or Brick

The same as the apple in regards to keeping focus on full body exercises. Although, cardio exercises will be less and Booty/Leg Day can be done with heavy weights and high resistance with the exception that the core is strong. For Booty Days focus on building your gluteus medius to create more hips (Abductor Exercises!).

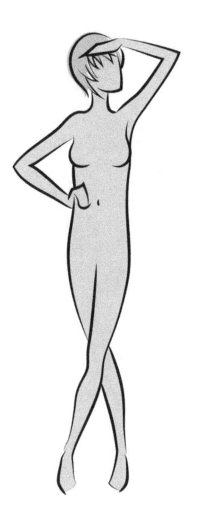

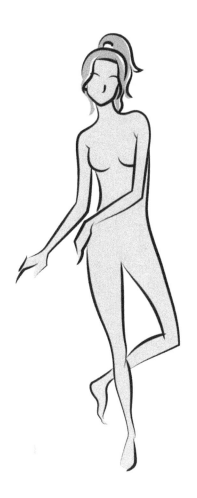

G. Petite

You will be able to perform any of the above body shape that you match with a focus on stretching. Strongly recommend resistance training combined with yoga. Body building can tend to make your muscles appear compact. This would make anyone with a petite frame look even shorter. Focusing on stretching exercises will make you longer and appear taller.

The ABC's of
M.I.L.F. Making

The ABC's of M.I.L.F. Making

Before we can go to the exercises, there are some "basics" that I'd like to go over for those of you who may be new to the exercises.

Feel free to skip these principles if you already are familiar with them.

Principles of Exercise
The F.I.T.T. Principle is an acronym for the basic principles of exercise.

You will be using these principles later to build your own exercise workout routines and program.

The "F.I.T.T." acronym stands for:
FREQUENCY:
How often you exercise

INTENSITY:
How hard you will exercise

TIME:
How long your exercise will be

TYPE:
What exercise you're doing

MILF Making requires a combination of Strength training with Full Body exertion to build your body whilst burning unwanted fat. These principles will be tailor based on building your body around your fitness and aesthetic priorities/lifestyle.

Basics: Fat loss (aka weightloss) & Muscle Building

The scale can be quite the trickster, since muscle weighs more than fat.

For instance, make a fist with one of your hands and look at it. This fist resembles approximately what one pound of muscle would look like. Now hold up two fists next to each other. Your two fists resemble what about a pound of fat would look like.

As you can see, fat takes up much more space than muscle does. I personally do not like to use the scale, except as a resource to find information to help gauge body fat percentage.

There are much better devices that can be used to gauge body fat, you would need to enter your height, age, and weight. Should you have access to those contraptions, I'd strongly recommend using them so you can know what you are starting with.

For now, in Self MILF Made, we'll be using your BMI along with your body shape to determine your workouts.

BMI = Body Mass Index.

This measurement of fat is based on your weight vs height.

To find your BMI, do the following:

1. Find your correct height.
2. Multiply your height in inches by itself.
3. Get your correct weight.
4. Divide your weight by your height.
5. Take that number and multiply by 703.
6. The number you end up with will be your BMI
7. Then use the scale below to find your BMI

Body Mass Index (BMI) Scale

<18	= **Underweight**
<18.5	= **Thin for height**
18.6 – 24.9	= **Healthy weight**
25 – 29.9	= **Overweight**
>30	= **Obesity**

Example:

Sally is 5ft 2inches
= 62 x 62 = 3844

She weights 120lbs.
120 / 3844 =

0.0312174817898023 x 703 = 21.94 BMI

Results:
Sally is within a healthy weight for her height

*Be sure to log down your BMI and the date!

As for muscle building, don't worry that you're going to look like a huge body builder after this program.

As women, we have higher estrogen levels than men. We would have to use muscle enhancing drugs, hormones, and workout for more than three hours daily to even get close to having a man's muscular physique.

With that said, do not be afraid to lift as heavy as you can. I like to tell my clients to take a favorite outfit or piece of clothing to use as their "Goal Tool".

Rather than using a scale, such as the ones found in most homes that do not measure body fat percentages, choose an outfit!

By using your favorite outfit or piece of clothing, you can put this on weekly to see where you are and how much more that needs to be done.

I personally just use my Hooter's shorts from when I was a Hooter's server. I keep a close eye on my "muffin top" and if my bottom starts to droop, then I'll know I need to focus on my Booty/Leg Days a little better.

Be sure to take a starting picture!

Increase Metabolism & Decrease Fat

Let's first start this part by knowing what metabolism is.

In a nutshell, metabolism is your body's ability to burn calories. The higher the BMI the more mass you have. Often times, the mass is not lean mass. When you have high BMI you might have more fatty tissue that you'd like.

Should your body's BMI be 25 or higher, chances are your ability to burn calories is much slower than if your BMI was lower.

The reason being is because your body does not have enough muscles to burn the calories, thus your body keeps unused calories and stores it as fat. Genetics and hormones released throughout your aging tells your body where to put this fat. For instance, cortisol aka the stress hormone, says to store the fat around your mid-section and your genetics may say to also store fat around your back if your body shape falls into the Ruler category.

Now, the next thing would be to know how to increase metabolism and thus decrease fat. We do this simply by increasing our overall body mass. Body mass includes your bones, organs, and lean muscle. With proper training, you can increase the density and strength of both your muscles and your bones.

Typically, at rest, a pound of muscle burns roughly 50 calories at rest. The more lean muscles you build, the more calories will be needed for them to exist, thus turning your body into a calorie burning machine.

Essentials

An essential piece to MILF Making is simple... Poise.

Keeping your posture and being mindful of form is very important. I always tell my clients that how you work out is how your body will build. So no slouching or hump backs, please!

Essential #1: CORE
In EVERYTHING you do, keep that core TIGHT.

Imagine a string that goes through the lower part of your spine and attaches from the inside of your belly button and pulls out through your lower spine. This "string" when pulled, draws your belly button to your spine. ("Belly Button to your Spine!") Vacuum Technique should also be practiced during all lifting exercises. This is where you keep your exhausted air out of your abs, bring the belly button to the spine, and keep your core tight. Practice by holding this for increments of 10 seconds at a time.

Essential #2: POSTURE
How you work out, is really how your body will build. Just think of those big guys in the gym with huge backs! They seriously need a training session on form. For now, I want you to imagine a string in the middle of your chest that goes straight up to the sky. Roll those shoulders back to a comfortable spot and lift up that chest using that imaginary string up towards the sky. Be sure to relax those shoulders (and your neck!) You should be sitting (or standing!) rather nicely with proper posture!

An exercise I have my clients do real quick when I see that they have rounded shoulders and poor posture is what I call "Rolling out the Shoulders". So when I tell my clients to "roll out their shoulders", this is what they do:

First hold your hands behind you, and clasp your fingers. Palms facing up, press your hands straight down, as in the following picture, on the right. Bring your chest up, roll your shoulders back, and tighten that core. Gently squeeze your shoulder blades together. Keep this isometric hold for 20 seconds at a time. Then gently release the hands and soften the shoulders. (You can do this as many times as you need.)

Left: Poor Posture
Right: Rolling Out the Shoulders

Put Essential #1 and Essential #2 together at all times, especially during exercises. If you can remember to hold #1 and #2 throughout the day for periods of time, muscle memory will eventually develop. Hold #1 really well, during most exercises. Just imagine someone is about to throw a basketball to your stomach. Do your very best to remember to keep your core tight!

Essential #3: FORM
Always use correct form.

When doing any sort of squat or lunge, perform what I like to call a "Toe Check". While down in your squat or lunge check to see if you can see your toes in front of you.

If you can only see your knee, chances are the majority of your body weight is being shifted to your knees. When this happens, you increase the risk of knee injury. Just make sure that your knee is aligned with your heel, and there is a very slight arch to your back.

I sometimes have to remind my clients to pop their butt out. "Pop it out!" (Oh, and please don't forget to engage your core and posture! Chest up! Belly button to the spine! Which pretty much is Essential #1 & #2)

Essential #4: WARM UP
Proper warm up. This is essential to avoid injury (and may help warm the body from becoming lightheaded from quick moves).

Typically, 5-10 minutes on a treadmill, elliptical, bike, walking, or even dynamic stretching are good warm up methods.

Essential #5: STRETCH
Dynamic Stretching is an awesome pre-workout.

This warms up your body whilst stretching. An example of dynamic stretching would be arm circles. Wide arm circles allow you to rotate your arms at full range of motion. 10 fwd/ 10 back, even add up to 2-5lbs of weight when you're ready.

Essential #6: CORRECT WEIGHTS, REPS, & SETS
Always use correct weights and repetition range.

All too many times, I see incorrect weights and reps being performed daily by gym goers who are uninformed of proper muscle building aka "toning".

If you use weights that are much too heavy you risk injury and if you use weights that are too light, you might not be doing anything for yourself "toning-wise".

Typically, we look at the percentage of your energy you exhaust to complete one repetition. We use this percentage along with knowledge of muscle tear and repair to find a weight and repetition selection for the desired workout.

On the following page, is the basic scale to know which weight is right for you.

We'll also be using various weights and combinations during different exercises, so this will at least give you a general idea.

Typically, when you are able to exhaust:

60%, you'd be able to get out 10 to 15 repetitions.

Anything above 80%, you'd only be able to complete 4-8 reps.

We'll mostly be using:

5 sets of 5 repetitions at 80% 1 rep max

3 sets of 12-20 repetitions @ 60% 1 rep max

This personalized program is just for you.

There will be tweaks with weight until we can get a nice consistent rhythm or until you plateau, or can't feel the burn.

Then you will increase or decrease weight as needed. Finding the correct weight is just one of the factors to personalizing this Self MILF Making program.

Training vs. Working Out

Especially, in the beginning of any fitness program, I've noticed so many people confusing training with working out.

The most simple way I can explain it is this:

When you are "working out", think of a run, a workout video, a cross training session, zumba session with girlfriends, etc.

When you are in training, you are IN TRAINING. You have to really think of yourself as an athlete at this point.

You are not just in training during that one hour of a workout, you are in Training Mode until you've reached your goal!

So when you are about to eat horribly or skip a workout, you've got to really remember that you are in training!

That way you will reach your goal.

Training can be one week or even months to years!

How long you want to be in training, is really up to you (and your personal trainer, if you have one!).

So now, you can visit your SMART goals and really determine how long you need to be in training mode.

Necessities
& Exercises

Necessities & Exercises

Although various exercises will be given for each muscle group, the use of equipment is entirely optional. These exercises can be done in the gym or in the privacy of your own home. (Please read the disclaimer, if you have yet to do so.) If you have access to a well-equipped gym that has muscle specific machines and you are not familiar with the exercises yet, I'd suggest that you utilize the gym (and even a trainer, if you can!).

If you do not have access to a trainer or a gym, just keep in mind of your form!!! You will do fine if you do not find yourself overcompensating your form to meet the completion of the exercise.

Some equipment options you might want to consider that will increase intensity are:

Exercise Ball/TRX Suspension Straps/BOSU
Dumbbells/Barbell/Resistance Bands with Handles
Workout Bench/Step Trainer
Yoga Mat & SMR Foam Roller (Highly recommended)
Jump Rope & Pull Up Bar

Highly suggested
Dumbbells: One heavy set & One light to medium set
2.5 lbs, 5 lbs, 8 lbs, 10 lbs, 15 lbs
(Advanced lifters can use 20 lbs or more)

If you have injuries or any inflexibility, chances are you won't keep your form and you might have to adjust the weight you are using or the exercise in its entirety.

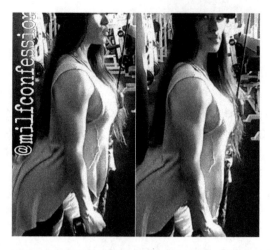

Exercises: Arms (All Upper Body)

These exercises include your shoulders, triceps, biceps, chest, and upper back muscles.

Upper Body: Warm up and Stretching

Various Arm Circles
None or Very Light Weight
Begin standing with your arms by your sides. Bring your arms up to align with your shoulders. Slow to medium speed, circle your arms forward 10 times /backward 10 times.
Add Variation: Palms facing up, palms facing down, wide arm circles, small arm circles, fist palms facing inward, palms facing out/fingers up

Arm Raises
Begin with your arms at your sides and raise them so that your arms are aligned with your shoulders in front of you, then bring your arms down to your sides and raise them up so that your arms are aligned with your shoulders on both sides. 10 times
Add Variation: Palms facing up, palms facing down, fist palms facing inward, palms facing out/fingers up

Arms Crossover
Begin with your arms at your sides and raise them so that your arms are aligned with your shoulders in front of you, then bring your arms down to your sides and raise them up so that your arms are aligned with your shoulders on both sides. 10 times
Add Variation: Palms facing up, palms facing down, fist palms facing inward, palms facing out/fingers up

Shoulder Roll Out
Begin with your arms at your sides and lift your shoulders to your ears then roll them back, down, and then to the front. Do this 10 times then rotate the other way, 10 times.

Triceps Stretch
Bring your right arm up and bend it at the elbow keeping your hand behind your neck. Take your left and and gently pull your right elbow to the left. Hold for about 10 seconds and repeat this on your left arm.

Arm Wall Stretch
Fully extend one arm out with your palm against a wall and fingers pointing back at shoulder level. Gently turn your body away from the wall. Hold this for up to 10 seconds. Then release and do other side.

Shoulder Stretch
Reach your right arm over your chest. Using your left hand pull your right elbow towards your left shoulder.

Wrist Flex
Stand with your arms straight in front of you, fingers up, and palms out. Take one hand and pull the other hand back gently pulling the fingers back towards you. Do the same with your fingers pointing down and palms in towards you.

Front Arm Raises
Begin standing with your arms down and in front of you. Palms in, raise your arms in front of you until your arms are at the same level as your shoulders. Bring your arms back down for one rep.

Light weights: 10 to 15 reps　　　Medium weights: 8 reps

Lateral Arm Raises
Begin standing with your arms down and in front of you. Palms in, raise your arms in front of you until your arms are at the same level as your shoulders. Bring your arms back down for one rep.

Light weights: 10 to 15 reps　　　Medium weights: 8 reps

Shoulder Press
Seated or standing with your arms up and bent at a ninety-degree angle on each side, palms can face either inward or out to the front of you. Squeeze your shoulders while lifting your arms straight up. Your arms should be fully extended at the end of one rep with your arms straight and close to your ears. Squeeze your shoulders and slowly release back to the starting position.

Light weights: 10 to 15 reps　　　Medium weights: 8 reps
Heavy weights: 4-6 reps

Arnold Press
Seated or standing with arms bent in close and in front of you with your palms facing inward to you. Squeeze your shoulders while lifting your arms straight up. As you extend your arms up, rotate your palms to face out. Your arms should be fully extended at the end of one rep with your arms straight, palms facing out, and arms close to your ears. Squeeze your shoulders and slowly release rotating your palms back to the starting position.

Light weights: 10 to 15 reps　　　Medium weights: 8 reps

Rotator Swings

With your arms out in front of you and bent at ninety degrees, palms facing upward. Chest up and belly button to your spine, keep your arms locked and close to your body. Slowly swing your arms open, then back to the starting position. Imagine the motion of saloon doors swinging open and close.
Light weights only: 10 to 12 reps

Upright Rows

Seated or standing with your palms down and arms down in front of you. Raise your arms only at your elbows, being sure to have your hands lower than your elbows. Do not bend your wrists. Squeeze your shoulders up to bring the elbows close to your head then slowly release your arms back down to the starting position.
Light weights: 10 to 15 reps
Medium weights: 8 reps
Heavy weights: 4-6 reps

Slow Angels

Seated or standing with your arms up at your sides and bent at a ninety-degree angle. Just as if you were starting with a shoulder press, extend your arms up so that they are close to your ears, then keep them slightly bent while very slowly coming down on your sides bringing them back in front palms up and back up in to the starting position for one repetition. Just think of making snow angels, but these are slow angels. This is a very effective isometric exercise. (The image shown on the left is of the exercise coming down. To see a shoulder press go to "Shoulder Press")
Light weights: 10 to 15 reps
Medium weights: 8 reps
Heavy weights: 4-6 reps

Chair or Floor Push Ups
Pushups can be down on the knees or on your toes. Just remember to bring the chest down while bending at the elbows and keeping your back straight and core tight.

Pull Ups
Very effective upper body workout. Do 10 at a time. If you cannot do 10, then do 1 and everyday do 1 until you realize you can do 2, then do 2 and so on.

High Planks Circles
In a push up position, on your hands and toes, slowly move your whole body in circles. As if you are drawing a big circle with your whole body. You will feel this in your shoulders, but this also works your core.

High Pike Push-ups
In a push up position, bring your bottom up high so now you look like a mountain with your bum in the air. Keep your hands close, bend at your elbows and only bring the crown of your head towards your hands. Push back up to starting position. You will also feel this in your shoulders, but also in your core and triceps.

Planks and Push Ups can be modified to increase intensity. Feet can be positioned spread apart, close together, on a chair, bench, or exercise ball, while the top of your body remains lower with your hands on the ground. In a Plank position on the floor, try holding up your left arm and right leg for 10 seconds or more, then switch!

Triceps (Tone these to avoid flabby arms!)

Using weights or resistance bands: Sit on an exercise ball to increase intensity when you're ready.

Punch Outs

Similar to triceps kickbacks, but instead of punching out behind you, you'll extend outwards to your sides. Lean forward, slight arch in lower back, core tight, and knees slightly bent. Bring one arm up so that it is parallel to the floor and in line with your spine. Bend that arm at the elbow while keeping your form. Punch out to fully extend the raised arm and squeeze your triceps.
Light weights: 10 to 15 reps / Medium weights: 8 reps

Overhead Triceps Extensions

Holding your arms up and hands over your head, bend your arms back at your elbows while keeping your elbows pointed forward. Then keep both of your upper arms close to your ears and fully extend your arms so that your hands are back over your head to the starting.
Light weights: 10 to 15 reps / Medium weights: 8 reps

Overhead Triceps Butterflies

Holding your arms up and hands over your head, bend your arms back at your elbows while keeping your elbows pointed forward. Then keep both of your upper arms close to your ears and fully extend your arms so that your hands are back over your head to the starting.
Light weights: 10 to 15 reps / Medium weights: 8 reps

Triceps Kickbacks

Similar to punch outs, but instead of punching out to the side of you, you'll extend out behind you. Lean forward, slight arch in lower back, core tight, and knees slightly bent. Bring one arm up so that it is parallel to your body and in line with your spine. Bend your arm at the elbow while keeping your form. Fully extend the raised arm and squeeze your triceps. Keep your other arm close to your body. (To assist keeping your form right, try bending over a bench or chair, holding yourself up on the seat with your hand without the weight.)
Light weights: 12 to 20 reps

Triceps: Using only body weight

One Arm Triceps Pushdown

Lie on your left side. Place your right palm on the floor in front of you. Hold your right shoulder with your left hand. Extend your right arm while pressing your right hand down, lifting up your upper torso until your right arm is fully extended. Release back to starting position.

Close Hands Push Ups

In push up position, keep your hands close to each other on the floor. Bend your arms at the elbows, pointing your elbows back, then push up to fully extend the arms. Beginners might find using the wall first and gradually make your way down to the floor.

Triceps Dips

On a chair, sit at the very end of the seat. Place each hand to the side of you, fingers gripping the chair and facing forward. Dip your body down until your arms are at a 90-degree angle. Make sure that your elbows stay in lined with your wrists. Push up your body until your arms are fully extended. Repeat. As you get stronger, place your feet further away. You may even add variation and intensity by lifting one foot at a time per set.

Beginners: 10 reps / Average: 20 reps / Advanced: 30+ reps

Biceps aka Your Guns

Using weights or resistance bands: Sit on exercise ball to increase intensity when you're ready.

Bicep Curls

With arms extended, down at your sides and palms facing out in front of you, bend at your elbows to curl in your arms. When bringing your arms back to the starting position pause half way down for one second then extend all the way down to complete your rep. Light weights: 10 to 15 reps / Medium weights: 8 reps / Heavy weights: 4-6 reps

Bicep Swings

Seated or standing with your arms bent at a 90-degree angle and at your sides with your palms facing up, begin to swing your arms forward to "close", keeping your shoulders square and your elbows close to your body. Swing back open with a very slight lift your chest. Repeat to complete your set.

Light weights: 10 to 15 reps
Medium weights: 8 reps
Heavy weights: 4-6 reps

Hammer Curls and Swings

These are done the same as regular bicep curls and bicep swings, with the exception of the position of the hands. The hammer position is done holding your handles of your resistance bands or dumbbells as if you are holding a hammer upright. Your palms should be facing inward towards your body.

Light weights: 10 to 15 reps
Medium weights: 8 reps
Heavy weights: 4-6 reps

Biceps: Using only body weight

Pull Ups Using a pull up bar, you can try variations where your palms face outward or inward. Beginners can consider using a chair nearby to assist them until they can lift their own body weight. In the beginning shoot for 1 pull up, then add another after you've done 1. Eventually, making it up to at least 10 per set a day

Chest

Chest Press

Lying with you back on a bench, exercise ball, or even along the length of a SMR Foam Roll, hold your resistance at chest level at your sides with your arms at a ninety-degree angle. With your palms facing out, press your resistance up over your chest, fully extending the arms, and slowly bring your arms back down to starting position.

Light weights: 10 to 15 reps   Medium weights: 8 reps
Heavy weights: 4-6 reps

Chest Flyes

If at the gym, try these using the cable machines. Try crossing your hands over and do a 3-in-1 pulse during the contraction before bringing your arms back.

Lying with you back on a bench, exercise ball, or even along the length of a SMR Foam Roll, hold your resistance at chest level at your sides with your arms at about a 135 degree angle. With your palms facing in, press your resistance up over your chest and slowly bring your arms back down to starting position.

Light weights: 10 to 15 reps   Medium weights: 8 reps
Heavy weights: 4-6 reps

Chest: Using only body weight

Push Ups

In push up position, keep your hands shoulder width apart to each other on the floor. Bend your arms at the elbows, pointing your elbows back, then push up to fully extend the arms. Beginners might find using the wall first and gradually make your way down to the floor.

Back

Wide Row

A good variation of this would be to lay over an exercise ball and use your feet to keep you balanced as you performed this exercise.

Standing with your legs hip width apart and slightly bent, bend over while keeping your core tight and shoulders rolled back. Hold your dumbbells or bands in front of you with your palms facing back, as if your hands are hanging from your arms aligned at your shoulders.

Start with your arms fully extended then bend your arms at your elbows to a 90-degree angle, bring your hands up to your chest, hold for 3 seconds, then bring your arms back down to the starting position for one repetition.

Light weights: 10 to 15 reps

Medium weights: 8 reps

Heavy weights: 4-6 reps

Bent Over Row

Standing with your legs hip width apart and slightly bent, bend over while keeping your core tight and shoulders rolled back. Hold your dumbbells or bands in front of you with your palms facing in, as if your hands are hanging from your arms aligned at your shoulders. Start with your arms fully extended then bend your arms at your elbows to bring your hands up and aligned with your belly button, hold for 1-3 seconds, then bring your arms back down to the starting position for one repetition.

Light weights: 10 to 15 reps

Medium weights: 8 reps

Heavy weights: 4-6 reps

Back Extensions
Start by lying on your stomach, bend your arms at your elbows and place your hands under your chin. Lift your chest up off the ground while lifting your legs straight up about two inches off the ground. Squeeze your glutes then release for one repetition.

Super Womans
Lying on your stomach, keep your arms straight and lift up your chest and your legs straight up about two inches off the ground. Squeeze your glutes then release for one repetition.

Good Mornings
Standing with your legs slightly wider than hips width apart, keep your hands behind your head. Bend only at your hips. Your shoulders should be kept rolled back and your core tight. Feel the stretching of your hamstrings then raise your body back into standing up right for one repetition.

Exercises: Booty (All Bottom Body Parts)

These exercises include your quadriceps, hamstrings, calves, and gluteal muscles aka da booty aka butt aka derrière.

Lower Body: Warm up and Stretching

High March

March in place but bring your knees up as high as you can, preferably passing your belly button. (Did you know that every time that you bring your knee up to your belly button, you are working your abs?!)

Plie Squats

Like sumo squats but bring your legs out as wide as possible for a nice stretch, bring your body down with your chest up, core tight, and bottom pointed down and back. Raise up and down for a nice warm up and dynamic stretch.

Calves Stretch
Stand with your feet together, extend one leg out and straighten out that leg. Slightly bend the supporting leg and bend your body down at your hips keeping your back straight. Try to grab your toes of the extended leg and feel the stretch from your calves all the way back up to your gluteal muscles. Hold this stretch on one side for about 10 seconds to 20 seconds at a time, then do the other leg.

Lateral Lunge Stretch
Stand with your legs pretty spread apart. Start with your right leg. Bend your right leg bringing your bottom down to the right. Make sure that your butt points back and down and that your right knee does not reach over your toes. Stand up straight, with your feet still in place and do the other side.

Leg Swings

Standing, take one leg and swing forward, backward, then outward. Pointing your toes towards you while your leg is in front of you will help stretch out your hamstrings. Kicking your heel towards your bum will help stretch out your quads. Do the same with the other leg, alternating 10 times. You can hold on to something for balance or just put your hands on your waist.

Quadriceps aka Your Lap
Using weights or resistance bands

Various Squats

Regular: Legs slightly wider than hips width apart
Sumo: Legs spread wide, keep knees pointed out in the same direction as toes and hips dip lower than knees

Stand with your legs slightly wider than hip width apart. Bend your knees towards the direction of your toes and bring your body down (as if to sit on a chair) to where your legs would be at least a ninety-degree angle. As you bring your body down, keep your chest up, shoulders rolled back, core tight, and butt back. Also make sure that your knees do not wobble or bow in and that they do not pass your toes while you are bringing your body down. Make sure your feet are flat on the ground, squeeze your glutes while going back up to standing for one repetition.

Beginners: 12 reps (Use only your own body weight, hands on hips, and gently squeeze elbows back to assist with form.)
Medium weights: 12 reps
Heavy weights: 8 reps

Split Squats

Stand with one leg in front of the other. While keeping your core tight, shoulders rolled back, and chest up, and buttocks popped back as you bring your body straight down by bending your back leg. With the bending of your back leg, your front leg will naturally follow. Look down at your leg in front to make sure that your knees are not covering your toes. Your legs should both be bent to a ninety degree angle. Squeeze your glutes coming back up to standing for one repetition on one side.

Beginners: 12 reps (Use only your own body weight, hands on hips, and gently squeeze elbows back to assist with form.)
Medium weights: 12 reps
Heavy weights: 8 reps

Forward Lunges

Alternative Lunges:
Backward: Instead of stepping forward, step backward.
Walking: Continue lunges by walking forward instead of bringing your foot back to the starting position.
Begin by standing with your feet roughly about hip width apart. Step forward with one leg and while keeping your core tight, shoulders rolled back, and chest up, and buttocks slightly popped back as you bring your body straight down by bending your back leg. With your back leg bending your front leg will naturally follow. Bend both legs to a ninety-degree angle. Do not allow your front knee to pass your toes. Squeeze your buttocks as you bring your front leg in by pushing yourself back up from your heel in to your starting position for one rep on one side.

Beginners: 12 reps (Use only your own body weight, hands on hips, and gently squeeze elbows back to assist with form.)
Medium weights: 12 reps
Heavy weights: 8 reps

Step Ups

Begin with one foot flat on a step in front of you and the other foot on the floor. While keeping your core tight, shoulders rolled back, and chest up, lift your whole body up to standing on that one foot on the step. Be sure to not allow your knee in front to pass your toes. You can bring your other foot up on to the step for stability, but I'd like for

you to eventually just bring the back leg up and tap your calves together and bring that leg back down to starting position for one repetition on one side.

Beginners: 12 reps (Use only your own body weight, hands on hips, and gently squeeze elbows back to assist with form.)

Medium weights: 12 reps

Heavy weights: 8 reps

Seated Leg Extensions

While seated in a chair, bring both feet up while squeezing at your quadriceps. Hold for 1-5 seconds. Bring your feet down to starting position for one repetition. (Be sure to sit up straight, please.) To add weight, hold a dumbbell between your feet or use resistance bands and do one foot at a time.

Beginners: 12 reps (Use only your own body weight.)

Medium weights: 12 reps

Heavy weights: 8 reps

Wall Sit

Stand with your back up against a wall. Lean against it as you slide your body down to bring your knees to about a 90-degree angle. Hold this position before you slide back up-

Beginners: less than 30 seconds

Average: 1 minute+

Advanced: 2 minutes+

Hamstrings
Using weights or resistance bands

Romanian Deadlifts

For SMM I prefer only Stiff legged Deadlifts aka Romanian Deadlifts. These not only hit your hamstrings the best, but hit the medius part of the glutes the best and help "create" hips for those who are lacking. Begin standing upright with your knees at a very slight bent. Keep your knees stiff like that and bend your body down at your hips. Keep your core tight, back straight with a slight lower back arch, and chest up. You should feel a nice pull in the hamstrings. Squeeze your glutes on your way up for one repetition.

Beginners: 12 reps (Use only your own body weight, hands on hips, and gently squeeze elbows back to assist with form.)
Medium weights: 12-15 reps
Heavy weights: 8 reps

Sumo Squats

Stand with your legs wide with your toes pointing outward but not completely to your sides. Bend your knees towards the direction of your toes and bring your body down to where your hips would be at level or lower than your knees. As you bring your body down, keep your chest up, shoulders rolled back, core tight, and butt back. Also make sure that your knees do not wobble or bow in and that they do not pass your toes while you are bringing your body down. Make sure your feet are flat on the ground, squeeze your glutes while going back up to standing for one repetition.

Beginners: 12 reps (Use only your own body weight, hands on hips, and gently squeeze elbows back to assist with form.)
Medium weights: 12 reps
Heavy weights: 8 reps

Leg Curl

On an exercise ball: Lie on your back with your heels on the ball. Bring your pelvis up and bend your legs, as if attempting to bring the ball towards your buttocks. Hold for 3-5 seconds and release back to the starting position for one repetition.

On a bench: Lie on your stomach with your legs half off the bench and place the weight between your feet. Keeping your legs still, bend your legs at your knees and bring the weight towards your glutes for a leg curl similar to a bicep curl (That's kind of funny because the medical term for your hammies is the "biceps femoris"!).

Using only body weight
Good Mornings

Standing with your legs slightly wider than hips width apart, keep your hands behind your head. Bend only at your hips. Your shoulders should be kept rolled back and your core tight. Feel the stretching of your hamstrings then raise your body back into standing up right for one repetition.

Abductor/Adductor
aka Your Outer and Inner Thighs

Sumo Hip Pulse

Start in a sumo squat position hips aligned with or lower than your knees, bring your body down while keeping your core tight, shoulders rolled back, and chest up, squeeze your knees outward as you bring your body up to about only an inch. Do not allow your knees to pass your toes. Bring your legs back in to starting position and body back down to starting position for one repetition

Beginners: 12 reps (Use only your own body weight and clasp your hands in front of you)

Medium weights: 12 reps (hold them together at your chest or up by your shoulders.)

Fire Hydrants
On your fours, bring one leg up to the side keeping it at a ninety-degree angle and bring it up so that its parallel to the ground. Hold for 1-3 seconds and bring it back down for one repetition.
No weights or Ankle weights may be ideal for this exercise.

Leg Crossovers
On your fours, fully extend one leg out so that it is straight. Bring that extended leg up and crossover the supporting leg. Bring the leg back to the starting position for one repetition.
No weights or Ankle weights may be ideal for this exercise.

Calves
Using weights or resistance bands

Calves Raises
Try pointing your toes in different directions for different sets to hit different parts of your calves.

With resistance bands or weights, simply stand tall on the balls of your feet then go back down for one repetition.
Beginners: 15 reps (Use only your own body weight, hands on hips, and gently squeeze elbows back to assist with form.)
Medium weights: 15-30 reps Heavy weights: 8-15 reps

Glutes aka da Booty
Using weights or resistance bands

Bridges
Lying on your back with your legs bent at your knees. Push your pelvis up pushing the weight through your heels on the floor, then back down for one repetition.
No weights or Ankle weights may be ideal for this exercise.

Lying Leg Lift
Lying on your back with your legs bent at your knees, extend on leg out. Push your pelvis up pushing the weight through the heel on the floor while keeping that extended leg up and out, then bring your pelvis down to the starting position for one repetition on one side.
No weight may be used or weight can be placed over your pelvis for added resistance.

Donkey Kickbacks
On all fours, extend one leg and bring it as high as you can without arching your back. Keep your core tight and your shoulders square.   Leading with your heel, squeeze your buttocks at the height of your extension then bring your leg back to starting position for one repetition on one side.
No weights or Ankle weights may be ideal for this exercise.

Pulse Variants
With any glute/leg exercises, you can increase mass where you need a pump, simply by added 2 or more pulses during the bottom of the set. For instance, say you're doing a squat, before you come up to complete your rep, do a three in one pulse rising your bottom about an inch up like you are going to stand, then go back down. Do this for the entire set. Only add weights when your form can handle it.

Exercises: Core & Cardio

Core exercises include your lower back and all the muscles that make up our abdominal wall. Before you continue though, I strongly encourage you to check if you have a Recti Split (please see below.) Also, I mainly focus on the lower abs on core day since that is where us women seem to have the most trouble and since we cover majority of the core on a daily with the vacuum technique.

Core
Using weights, resistance bands, and exercise ball.

*Plank
Variations: On your palms, on your forearms, with your feet elevated on an exercise ball, bench, or a chair. Keep your body straight with your palms on the ground and aligned with your shoulders. Your heels should be over your toes and your core tight. Be sure to not allow your abdomen to droop down and hollow out your lower back. Keep that core tight by tucking in your pelvis and drawing in your belly button. Hold this position for a nice isometric hold for at least 1 minute.

*Plank Twist whole core
Keep your body straight with your palms on the ground and aligned with your shoulders. Your heels should be over your toes and your core tight. Do not allow your abdomen to droop down and hollow out your lower back. Dip one side of your hip towards the ground and then back up and then dip the other side of your hip towards the ground and then bring it back up for one repetition.

*Side Incline with Reach whole core

Up in plank position, go on one arm and fully extend the other arm up allowing you to be in a side plank. Reach up with the extended arm, then under your rib cage while in this side plank. Bring your arm back up for one repetition.

*Leg Drops lower abs

Lying on your back with your arms up, bent up, and hands behind your head, begin this exercise with your legs up at a ninety-degree angle. Keeping your legs at a ninety-degree angle, drop one so that the heel touches the ground or just far enough that your lower back does not begin to arch up.

*Reverse Crunches lower abs

Lying on your back with your arms at your sides, lift your legs up to a ninety-degree angle. Lift your legs and your butt up off the ground, bringing your knees up to your chest for a reverse ab crunch. Bring your butt back down on the ground while keeping your legs locked in that 90 degree angle for one repetition.

Lying Windshield Wipers obliques and lower abs
Lying on your back with your arms fully extended at your sides, extend both of your legs straight up or keep them bent at a ninety-degree angle. Bring both legs to one side then lift back up and down to the other side for one repetition.

Russian Twists obliques, upper, and lower abs
Sitting up with your knees bent, slowly bring your upper body down so that your whole body is that of a V shape. Clasp your hands together and twist your body to touch both your hands to one side of your body, then the other side. To increase the intensity of this exercise, raise both of your feet off the ground and put weight in your hands.

+**Hip Ups** lower abs
Lying on your back with your arms bent at the elbows and hands under your head, fully extend both of your legs straight up. Flex your feet and raise your butt off the ground in the direction of your heels. You know that you're doing this right if you're able to get your hips up about an inch up off the ground, if you've never done these before.

+*****Kegal/Pelvic Tilts** pelvic floor and foundation for lower abs.
Lying on your back with your arms bent at the elbows and hands under your head, keep your feet down but your legs bent up. Squeeze your kegal muscle as you tilt your pelvis in. Hold this for 10 seconds for one repetition, increase the holding time as you progress. (If you do not know what your kegals are, it is the muscle that you squeeze when you want to stop going pee. To find this muscle, try to stop your urine during mid-stream. There! You found it!)

*Safe for Recti Split / +Lift head and shoulders during exercise to engage upper abs

Diastasis Recti aka Recti Split Test

If you were to look at a six pack, I want you to take notice of a line that goes right down the middle. This line is called the Linea Alba and is the connective tissue for your "six pack". Often times this tissue can become weak due to pregnancy or even just from being overweight. When this tissue is weak it can stretch out, allowing your soft tissue in your abdomen to protrude out. When this happens, you might have what is called a Diastasis Recti Split.

If you unknowingly have a recti split, going directly into abdominal workouts, like sit ups, could actually make matters worse. Do not worry if you find out that you have a recti split as it is repairable. (Both men and women can suffer from this!)

Recti Split Test:
1. Lie on your back with your knees bent.
2. Lift up your head off the ground as if going in for a crunch.
3. Look at your abs and run your fingers down the middle line of your abs.
4. Check to see if you can fit your finger or fingers through the middle; or if there is bulging coming out along any part of that line.

-      If you are able to get three fingers in between your "six pack", chances are that you have a Recti Split.
-      If you do, please only do the exercises noted with a "*" until the split is only able to fit one finger. If you can feel the line and are unable to fit more than one finger or barely two, chances are that you do not have a Recti Split and can proceed with all the core exercises.

Cardio Suggestions

Burpees
Begin in a push up position, do one push up; Jump your feet in towards your hands that are still on the ground, then jump straight up. When you come back down, put your hands down at the sides of your feet and jump back into push up position for one repetition.

Tuck Jumps
Stand with your legs hip width apart. Bend your arms at a ninety-degree angle with your palms facing down. Jump up so that your butt points back and your knees tuck up under your palms. If you can jump and bring your knees to your chest, then you just might be advanced. Continue to jump towards your chest the best you can if you can't.

Mountain Climbers
Begin in a high plank position, and bring one knee to your chest so that foot is also under your chest. Keep your other leg fully extended behind you. Then switch legs for one repetition.

Jump Lunges
Begin in a lunge position with one leg in front of the other. Then thrust up and switch legs in midair. Keep in mind of your form and core as to encourage your stabilizing muscles to assist you.

Jump Rope
Jump Rope for 30 seconds to a minute at a time.

Jumping Jacks

Begin standing with your arms by your sides. Jump out to bring your legs out to your sides and your arms up over your head. Jump up again as you bring your arms down and legs back together.

Sumo Jumps

In a sumo squat position, keep your legs out, and just jump from your toes. This works great for glutes and calves! One of my favorites during leg day.

High March n' Hold

Begin to march in place bringing your knees high above your belly button with every step. After 5 single high steps, hold up one knee for 5 seconds. You can also do a light jog with high knees, faster you do this the faster your heart rate will go up. Normally, I have clients do this 5-10 times, depending on their level of fitness.

Cardio Machines are awesome! Just do not plan on staying on there for the whole duration of your workout. Adding various intervals of different exercises can increase muscle tone and over all fat loss.

So a great cardio machine workout could be 1 minute run and a 1 minute plank!

Stretching, & SMR

Stretching out worked muscles is the best thing besides actually working them out for growth.

Stretching them out allows the blood to flow easier throughout the muscles for repair and growth besides, of course, sleeping.

I am not going to go too far in to stretching exercises, but if you feel that you are super tighter in some areas you might even want to consider Self Myofascial Release or SMR.

This is where you take a foam roller or even a tennis ball (just something firm) and kneed your tight muscles out. Kind of like a deep tissue massage that you can get at a massage parlor.

A word of caution, when using SMR you may feel mild to excruciating pain, depending on the severity of the tightness in your muscles. I suggest holding a stretch 15-20 seconds before releasing it.

"Give so much to the improvement of yourself, that you don't have time to criticize others." ~Jim Rohn

@milfconfessions

Saggy & Stretchmark Skin Tips

1. Hydrate!!! One rule of thumb as to how much water you should consume: Shoot for at least 1/3 of your weight in ounces to drink. So let's say you weight 150lbs, 1/3 of that is 50, you'd want to drink at least 50 ounces of water daily! Divide that by 1- 8oz glass, that's at least 6-7 glasses of water you need to drink daily!

2. Derma Roller!!! Use this inexpensive method to penetrate the layers of skin so that products like coco butter, vitamin E, and Hyaluranic acid can easily access where collagen is made!

3. Exfoliate!!! Regular exfoliation allows the removal of old skin to make room for new skin!

4. Use real products! Try to stay away from brand name products that fill their bottles with ingredients that do more harm than good! Opt for straight ingredients you can purchase ala cart from a vitamin store! Hyaluranic Acid, Vitamin E, Jojoba Oil, Cocoa Butter, Menthol Vapor Rub, and Coconut Oil are awesome for both skin tightening and stretchmark fading.

"I think that whatever size
or shape body you have,
it's important to embrace it and get down!

The female body is something that's so
beautiful. I wish women would be proud of
their bodies and not diss other women for
being proud of theirs!"

~Christina Aguilera

Creating Your Very Own Program To Shape YOUR Best Shape...

Now that we've made it past the exercises section of this book...

(Just so you are aware, you will learn about more exercises along the way as there are plenty more available on-line and through people in your life that already are aware of these exercises. Do not fret!

Rule of thumb with **any** exercise: PLEASE make sure you keep your neck neutral, core tight, and posture on point at all times!!!

Remember, how a body works out, that's the way it will build!

Should you feel that your form is being compromised in anyway, it probably might be a good idea to do something else.

Something else, could easily mean, go less in weight, or try a different exercise that would hit the muscle that you are targeting) ...now, it's time to put everything together.

Step 1: Revisit your SMART Goals. Remember how many days you said that you could commit to working out?

Step 2: Which body shape did you find that your own body shape related to?

Step 3: Use the next page to find and build your workout split.

Then we'll move on to how hard you should be working out according to your fitness level and BMI...

A. Hourglass

3 Days:
Day 1- Bottom
Day 2- Core
Day 3- Arms

4 Days:
Day 1- Bottom
Day 2- Core
Day 3- Arms
Day 4- Core

5 Days:
Day 1- Bottom
Day 2- Core
Day 3- Arms
Day 4- Core
Day 5- Bottom

B. Triangle

3 Days:
Day 1- Bottom
Day 2- Core
Day 3- Arms

4 Days:
Day 1- Bottom
Day 2- Core
Day 3- Arms
Day 4- Bottom

5 Days:
Day 1- Bottom
Day 2- Arms
Day 3- Bottom
Day 4- Core
Day 5- Bottom

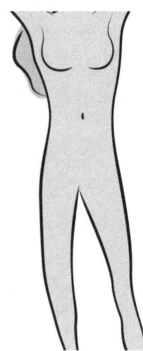

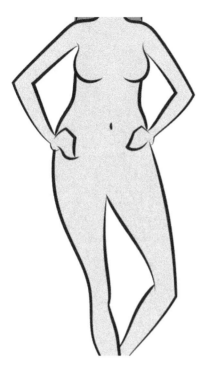

C. PEAR
3 Days:
Day 1- Arms
Day 2- Core
Day 3- Bottom
4 Days:
Day 1- Arms
Day 2- Core
Day 3- Bottom
Day 4- Core
5 Days:
Day 1- Arms
Day 2- Bottom
Day 3- Core
Day 4- Arms
Day 5- Bottom

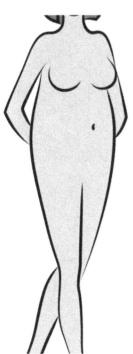

D. APPLE
3 Days:
Day 1- Bottom
Day 2- Core
Day 3- Arms
4 Days:
Day 1- Bottom
Day 2- Core
Day 3- Arms
Day 4- Bottom
5 Days:
Day 1- Bottom
Day 2- Arms
Day 3- Bottom
Day 4- Core
Day 5- Bottom

E./F. RULER/BRICK

3 Days:
Day 1- Bottom
Day 2- Core
Day 3- Arms

4 Days:
Day 1- Bottom
Day 2- Core
Day 3- Arms
Day 4- Bottom

5 Days:
Day 1- Bottom
Day 2- Arms
Day 3- Bottom
Day 4- Core
Day 5- Bottom

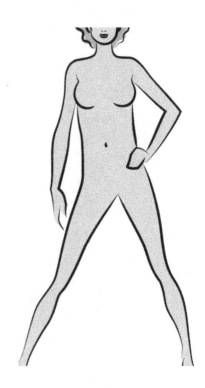

G. PETITE

You will be able to perform any of the above body shape focus exercise routines that you match with a concentration on stretching. I'd focus on stretching exercises that will help make you appear leaner and taller. Hypertrophy or muscle growth may give the appearance of looking stumpy, so just be mindful of your workouts and how your body is building.

How Much Cardio Should I Do?

Depending on how much fat we are trying to get rid of will determine how much cardiovascular activity you should be doing on a weekly basis.

I have found the following to be most effective with my clients: Incorporate <u>at least</u> 3 days of cardio in your weekly workout schedule, along with the following if you...

...are underweight
Length: 20-25 minutes of
Intensity: Med @ low speed

...are at a healthy weight
Length: 20-35 minutes of
Intensity: Med-High @ low-med speed

...are overweight
Length: 30-45 minutes of
Intensity: Low-Med-High @ low-med speed

To calculate your target heart rate: Take your age - 220, Take that number and multiply it by .70 (this is the med/max rule of thumb for weight loss and endurance).

For instance, Sam is 40 years young, and over weight.
40 subtracted from 220= 180,
180 x .70 = 126

Sam should try to keep her heart rate steady at 126 for at least 15 to 25 minutes in the beginning and work her way up (but no more than 45 minutes).

How Intense Should My Workouts Be?

Remember how we checked your BMI earlier?

We are going to revisit your information and use it to see how intense your workouts could be.

Use your BMI findings and follow the intensity scale below.

This intensity scale is merely a gauge to suggest the level of intensity based on your BMI.

If at any point you feel that you need to increase or decrease the intensity, use the scale to assist you.

You will know that you need to **decrease** when you feel that you are winded, have difficulty catching your breath, or if your form is being compromised by the end of your first set.

You will know that you need to **increase** your intensity when you don't feel anything by the end of your third set.

(All too often, people will think that the weight that they are starting at is much too light. Then when they get to the second and third set, they are unable to complete the set with proper form or reps. This is a sign that it's too much for them.)

I strongly recommend that you pace yourself.

The last thing we'd want is for you to burn out and not complete your transformation

Body Mass Index (BMI) Scale

<18   = Underweight
<18.5   = Thin for height
18.6 – 24.9 = Healthy weight
25 – 29.9   = Overweight
>30   = Obese

Intensity Based on BMI

Underweight
Cardio Reps per Set: 5, 10, 15
Timed sets: 10-15 seconds
Cardio Activity: 20-25 minutes of
High resistance as you are comfortable with @ low speed

Example: On a treadmill with settings 2.2mph / 12-15 incline

Healthy weight
Cardio Reps per Set: 15, 20, 30+
Timed Sets: 30+ seconds
Cardio Activity: 20-45 minutes of
High resistance as you are comfortable with @ low-med speed

Example: On a treadmill with settings 2.2mph / 12-15 incline

Overweight, and Obese
Cardio Reps per Set: 5, 10, 15
Timed sets: 10-15 seconds
Cardio Activity: 15-45 minutes of
High resistance as you are comfortable with @ med speed

Example: Walk for 1 minute then jog for 1 minute for 30 min total.

Workout Formulas

GENERAL DAY
1. 3-7 minutes Warm up (Treadmill, Dynamic Exercises)
2. 5 minutes Optional Additional Stretching (Dynamic)
3. 30-60 minutes Resistance Workouts (See Below for Arms, Legs, and Core Days)
4. 25 minutes (or more depending on your cardio needs) Cardio Burn Out
5. 5 minutes Stretching Finish

ARM DAY
1. Choose 3- 5 exercises.
2. Do singles set of that exercise in Medium to Light weight
3. Superset with 4-6 reps of Medium to Heavy weight
4. Choose a complimenting cardio OR single tempo exercise.

BOTTOM DAY
1. Choose 3- 5 exercises.
2. Do singles set of that exercise.
3. Superset with a *Pulse 3-in-1 set.
4. Choose a complimenting cardio OR single tempo exercise.

CORE DAY
1. Choose 3- 5 exercises.
2. Do singles set of that exercise
3. Choose a complimenting cardio exercise to Superset with
4. Choose a BMI considered cardio activity

[EXAMPLE]:
ARM DAY for PEAR Body w/LOW BMI

Set 1

Bicep Curls (Regular Grip) - 8lbs dumbbells / 12 reps

Bicep Curls (Hammer Grip) - 8lbs dumbbells / 12 reps
Good Morning w/ Back Row - 8lbs dumbbells / 12 reps

Set 2

Hammer Swings - 8lbs dumbbells / 12 reps

Shoulder Press - 8lbs dumbbells / 12 reps
Plank - 1 Minute

Set 3

Triceps Butterflies - 8lbs dumbbells / 12 reps

Triceps Extensions - 8lbs dumbbells / 12 reps
Push Ups On BOSU - 10

Repeat 3 times

EXTRA: Finish with 20 Minutes Low Intensity Cardio, ex: Treadmill at high incline and moderate to brisk stride.

[EXAMPLE]:
BOTTOM DAY for APPLE Body w/HIGH BMI

Set 1

Sumo Squats - only body weight / 12 reps

Sumo Squats Pulse - only body weight / 12 reps
Plank - 1 Minute

Set 2

Alternating Forward Lunge - only body weight / 12 reps

Alternating Backward Lunge - only body weight / 12 reps
High Knees March - 1 Minute

Set 3

Chair Sitdown & StandUps - only body weight / 12 reps

Wall Sit - only body weight / to fail
Mountain Climbers - 10

Repeat 3 times

EXTRA: When completing a task, but your BMI is high, PLEASE take it easy. What may seem easy to others may be super difficult because of limited range of motion. Do not fret, this is temporary. Stay the course, and speedy mountain climbers will be yours!

[EXAMPLE]:
CORE DAY for RULER Body w/HIGH BMI

Set 1

High Knee March - only body weight / 12 reps

Plank - 30 Seconds to 1 Minute

Set 2

Leg Drops - 12 reps

Mountain Climbers - 12 reps

Set 3

Jumping Jacks - only body weight / 12 reps

Chair Sit Stands - only body weight / 12 reps

Repeat 4 times

EXTRA: Please note that any transformation will be most noticeable with a clean diet.

Suggested Nutrition & Supplement Basics

The following page shows general suggestions based on what my clients and I do. These are not mandatory, they are merely suggestions.

Nutrition Basics...

* NEVER eat more than your balled up fist size in a single sitting.

* Know what Simple Sugars are and leave them for the simple minded... except for birthday parties and well deserved cheat days! (Simple sugars are mostly man made- breads, desserts, pastas, etc.)

* Eat your daily protein needs. Generally, 1 gram of protein for every pound of weight you are currently. You can add more if you are lifting more. But do not consume more than needed if you are not going hard in your training, protein can turn into fat, too!

* Eat your daily fiber needs. Generally, 25 grams of fiber per day, according to the Institute of Medicine. I find doing this makes great for a itty bitty waistline!

*Eat Low and Complex Carbs on Upper Body Days & High Complexed Carbs on Lower Body Days- Pizza and Spaghetti are ok if you are already at your goal weight.

* Awesome Snacking: VEGETABLES!!!

* Replace simple foods in your home with healthier options and fresh foods. and *Stay away from additives, preservatives, hormones, food coloring, etc. They wreak havoc on your body as a whole.

Supplement Basics...

* Protein Shakes
Aids in meeting your protein needs. Time friendly. Great for right after a workout!

* Pre-Workout: I prefer coffee.

* BCAAs
Branch Chain Amino Acids are great for muscle repair. Can also be used during a detox.

*Creatine
Great for bulking!!! Let's say you're trying to build your legs, take a serving of this before your training session! Use in moderation and only as needed!

* Women's Mutli-Vitamin
Formulated for women means special attention to our feminine needs.

* Omega Oils: 3, 6, 9
Omega 3 is best for lowering the rist of chronic diseases, cancers, and needed for overall health and wellness. Omega 6 & 9 in moderation is ok, too much of these two can have adverse health affects.

* Antioxidants: My favorite is Astaxanthin & going out into the Sun for 15 minutes and get natural Vitamin D!

* MSM, Chondroitin, Glucosamine, & Hyaluranic Acid:
GREAT for aging joints!

Final Notes...
& Thank you!

Dear Fellow Self M.I.L.F. Maker,

I congratulate you on your quest! I practically gave you everything that I incorporate in pretty much the routines I prepare for my clients (and myself!). But before I let you go, there are a few notes I'd like to leave you with:

*Please seek your medical provider for any potential problems regarding if your health may be an issue. I also suggest that you seek attention of a personal trainer to assist you and guide you in the beginning and or throughout your Self M.I.L.F. Making process, if you are not already familiar with form and technique.

*Please note that the exercises can be combined (just think squat and shoulder press on your way up). Also, the exercises provided are pretty basic, but very effective. Should you know of other exercises that are effective for working a certain muscle group, feel free to incorporate it in your program.

*Normally, your complete workouts could range from 1-2 hours, which may include a 30 minute cardio session, depending on how much time you have to keep consistent.

*Begin the week with your weakest area. For instance, if you have a Pear shaped body, your weakest areas may be your arms and core.

*Be prepared to switch up your program every 4-5 weeks. This time enables you to get stronger and progress towards a permanent transformation and avoids plateauing. One pound of muscle takes
about 4-6 weeks to build! And remember we need muscles to build up our metabolism to truly lose that fat for good.

*Also, a rule of thumb if you're working on bringing your BMI down, (with proper nutrition and exercise) expect to lose 1-2 pounds or 1% of your overall body weight. This can safely be done every week.

*Proper nutrition requires baby steps in the right direction. Everyday eliminate anything that may cause inflammation one day at a time. For instance, replacing your cow's milk for a plant based milk, like almond milk would be a great first baby step. Another good one is replacing your white rice with brown rice. (Don't worry "Self M.I.L.F. Made in the Kitchen" is in the works... So please stay tuned!)

*Drink plenty of water! Another rule of thumb is to drink 60-80% of your body weight in ounces of water. If you don't like the taste, try squeezing lemons or even oranges to bring flavor to your water. I
use a shaker bottle and keep sliced lemon in it as I refill it throughout the day with my gallon.

*Don't forget to rest! On average, you don't want to go three days in a row without exercising. Although, you do want to rest your muscles by skipping one to two days. While that muscle group is
repairing at rest, you can work on the other. Say you had legs yesterday, then do arms today!

*One last note... Fitness is a lifestyle and not a trend. Just like good hygiene when you wake up first in thing in the morning when you brush your teeth. It won't matter if you're hung over until 3pm, you will brush your teeth, because hygiene is important to you. The same goes for fitness. Fit it in and make it a habit. They say it takes three months of constantly doing something to make it a habit.

Again, I'd like to congratulate you for taking matters into your own hands. It gives me great pleasure and satisfaction to see fellow women confident, happy, and proud of themselves. We deal with so much on a daily that the last person to give us any heck would and should be ourselves. We might as well take care of #1.

Oh, and please remember that it took time to get your body to where it is now and it will take some time to get it to where you want it to be. So give it time! You got this!

In good health, love, and light...

xoxo,

Dana

P.S.
I love connecting with my readers/clients,
please feel free to add me on:
Instagram: MilfConfessions for personal
Instagram: SelfMilfMade for more tips and tricks
Twitter: selfmilfmade
Facebook: bodyreignfit
Comment: "Self Milf Made!" and I will follow you back!

M. I. L. F.
Mom Into Lifting & Fitness

Should you have any questions regarding your personal Self Milf Made program, you can email me directly:
danalareine@gmail.com

I will answer emails in the order they are received.

Promotional codes for discounts on future products will be available only to my readers.

Please be sure to register your email on www.bodyreign.com.

Cheers to being Self M.I.L.F. Made!!!

CPSIA information can be obtained
at www.ICGtesting.com
Printed in the USA
LVHW012039180520
655843LV00006B/585